Does It Pay to Get an MBA?

Does It Pay to Get an MBA?

Evidence from the *Forbes*
business school rankings

With spreadsheets for estimating the value of
full-time and part-time MBA degrees

by

Ronald N. Yeaple, Ph.D.[1]

---

[1] Former Associate Dean at the Roy E. Crummer Graduate School of Business at Rollins College.

Published by
The Center for Research in Management Education
Orlando, FL
www.crme.org

Printed by
Xerographic Digital Printing
Orlando, FL
www.xerocopy.com

ISBN 0-9787541-0-7

Second edition

To Bev

CONTENTS

CENTER FOR RESEARCH IN MANAGEMENT EDUCATION

The Center for Research in Management Education is dedicated to analyzing current trends and opportunities in graduate management education, and to making recommendations for improvement. Its focus is on the process of educating future managers and entrepreneurs, in the belief that intellectual assets—brainpower, not physical or financial assets—have become the defining criteria for business success in the 21st Century.

Ronald N. Yeaple, Ph.D., is Executive Director. Mark W. Johnston, Ph.D., Associate Director and Gerry Chair Professor of Marketing and Ethics; and Keith L. Whittingham, Ph.D., Director of Research, Visiting Associate Professor of Management Science and former Associate Dean, both at the Roy E. Crummer Graduate School of Business at Rollins College, provide the Center with academic and professional leadership. The three principals of the Center have extensive experience teaching MBA students, and each has received numerous awards for outstanding teaching.

The Center for Research in Management Education is an independent research organization funded in part by a grant from the Crummer Graduate School of Business at Rollins College.

ABOUT THE AUTHOR

From July 2001 to May 2002, Ronald N. Yeaple was Associate Dean at the Roy E. Crummer Graduate School of Business at Rollins College in Winter Park, Florida and later was appointed Distinguished Professor of Marketing. While Associate Dean, he concentrated on marketing the Crummer School with the objective of increasing the size and quality of the MBA applicant pool. Applications to the full-time MBA programs increased 60%, and the average GMAT score of the incoming MBA classes increased by 35 points.

Prior to joining the Crummer School, Dr. Yeaple served for 26 years as Executive Professor of Business Administration at a Top 25 business school, the Simon Graduate School of Business at the University of Rochester. A four-time winner of the Simon School's Superior Teaching Award, Dr. Yeaple taught courses on *Internet Marketing, E-Commerce, Marketing Management, Marketing Research, The Strategic Management of Technology, Control Theory,* and *Business Policy.*

He also founded and served as the first director of the Simon School's Business Innovation Team, which was funded by the New York State Science and Technology Foundation to sponsor teams of students and faculty who analyzed markets and developed business strategies for high-tech startup companies.

Dr. Yeaple is the author of three previous books, *The MBA Advantage* (Adams, 1994), *The Success Principle* (Macmillan, 1997), and *Net Profit: Successful Internet Marketing Strategies* (1999). These books have been cited and reviewed in major periodicals including *The Wall Street Journal*, *Business Week*, *Canadian Business*, *Forbes*, and *The Economist*, in academic and professional journals such as the *Journal of Marketing* and the *CPA Journal*, in various career books, on radio and television and on the Internet, and in leading newspapers throughout the world.

In February 2000, the research methodology introduced in *The MBA Advantage* was adopted by *Forbes* as the basis for its biennial published survey that ranks the top business schools by the economic value of their MBA degrees. Dr. Yeaple has also authored journal articles and book chapters in both biomedical engineering and business management. He has consulted with more than 50 firms in marketing and new product planning, and has served on a number of boards of directors. He holds five patents in acoustics, biomedical engineering and electronic publishing and has one patent pending.

Prior to joining the Simon School faculty, Dr. Yeaple was Executive Vice President of the Ritter Company, a biomedical products firm with sales of $30 million. He began his career as Product Manager of Consumer Products for Stromberg-Carlson stereophonic equipment. A high point of his early career was designing a custom stereo system for President John F. Kennedy, which he personally installed in the second-floor living quarters of the White House.

In addition to bachelor and master's degrees in electrical engineering from Cornell University, Dr. Yeaple holds a PhD in electrical engineering and an MBA from the University of Rochester.

INTRODUCTION

"Dad, I've been thinking about getting an MBA…again." My daughter Susan, a desktop publishing specialist in the executive offices of a major publisher, reached into her briefcase and pulled out a couple of business school catalogs.

"I'd really like to have an MBA, but it just seems so expensive. Is it worth it to go full-time? Or should I keep working and attend a part-time MBA program? Does it pay to get an MBA?"

For many years I was a faculty member at a top-ranked business school, where I had been teaching marketing courses and doing research on how business schools are ranked by *Business Week* and other publications.

Prompted by Susan's question, I began to research the value of the MBA degree, and in 1994 I authored a book, "The MBA Advantage," that introduced a new method for evaluating and ranking the top business schools by the economic value of their MBA degrees—a method later adopted by *Forbes* magazine for its biennial business school rankings.

Attending a full-time MBA program is a major decision, requiring the investment of two years and as much as $150,000 or more (including foregone salary). Is it worth it? And what about less expensive alternatives, such as part-time MBA programs and Executive MBA programs and online programs. Are they worth it?

This book, "Does It Pay to Get an MBA?," examines these questions in the light of the latest research, building on the fundamental concepts of "The MBA Advantage." While financial gain may not be your primary reason for getting an MBA, it's worth finding out whether the degree will pay for itself in a reasonably short time.

Topics in this new book include a review of the explosive growth in MBA degrees awarded over the past three decades, despite numerous magazine and newspaper articles over the years forecasting the imminent demise of the MBA. A discussion of the reasons for pursuing an MBA is followed by an analysis of recent articles—by business school professors!—claiming the MBA has no value, and why they are completely wrong.

Using data from the 2005 *Forbes* business school survey, the value of both full-time and part-time MBA degrees is explored, along with the advantages and limitations of each kind of program.

A new trend is emerging for those interested in full-time programs—after years of insisting that applicants have 3 to 5 years of pre-MBA work experience, a number of leading business schools are now accepting students with little or no work experience.

Analysis of the *Forbes* data also provides a unique view of how some schools are providing extra value to their students through superb teaching. And one of the most interesting findings of this new research is quantitative evidence that part-time programs generally provide higher financial gains than full-time programs at the same schools.

Finally, the subject of business school rankings is analyzed, with the finding that some of the rankings from even the most respected magazines and newspapers are biased and potentially misleading for prospective students trying to choose a business school.

In writing this book, I've tried to keep it brief and concentrate on the essentials, so you can decide whether it pays *you* to get an MBA.

What are my qualifications to write about this important subject? In 1999, I retired from 26 years of full-time teaching at a leading business school, having won the school's Superior Teaching Award four times. Subsequently I served as Associate Dean and Distinguished Professor of Marketing at the Roy E. Crummer Graduate School of Business at Rollins College in Winter Park, Florida. Most of my career has been spent teaching and advising MBAs.

Prior to becoming a business school faculty member, I was Executive Vice President of a $30 million medical products company while still in my early thirties—an accomplishment that was due in large part to having obtained an MBA after completing my engineering degree.

What motivated *me* to get an MBA? As a young engineer working in product planning, I kept losing arguments to the accountants, who shot down my business proposals as being unprofitable. I decided to pursue an MBA so I could understand their objections and argue more intelligently. With my new MBA skills I started winning those arguments, and my career took off.

As for Susan, she went on to earn her MBA in the Executive MBA program at Rollins College. I asked her recently whether it was worth it. She said with great enthusiasm that it was.

Ronald N. Yeaple, Ph.D.
Orlando, Florida

ACKNOWLEDGEMENTS

My thanks to the many people who encouraged me to develop my first book, "The MBA Advantage," and to those who supported my plan to update this work.

In particular, I would like to thank Craig McAllaster, Dean of the Crummer Graduate School of Business at Rollins College and Steve Gauthier, Associate Dean. I would also like to thank Senior Associate Dean Robert Hansen and Associate Dean David Pyke at the Tuck School at Dartmouth College, Dean Mark Zupan at the Simon School at the University of Rochester, Professor Tom Dyckman at the Johnson School at Cornell University, and Professor Mark Johnston and Professor Keith Whittingham, both at the Crummer School at Rollins.

My thanks also to Kurt Badenhausen at *Forbes* magazine, Ron Alsop at *The Wall Street Journal*, and Larry Rudner at the Graduate Management Admission Council; Jana Allen, Alice Argeros, Jacqueline Brito, Erin Pianko, Anne Roberts, and Nicole Vickers at the Crummer School at Rollins College; and Yiary Lopez and Rain Woodall at Xerographic Digital Printing.

Finally, I would like to thank my many successful MBA students at the University of Rochester and at Rollins College for helping me understand why it pays to get an MBA.

PART I

THE VALUE OF THE MBA DEGREE

1

THE MASTER OF BUSINESS ADMINISTRATION DEGREE: A HIGHER EDUCATION SUCCESS STORY

The growth of the Master of Business Administration degree has been a major success story in higher education over the past three decades. Since 1970, the number of master's degrees in business has grown by a factor of nearly 7 times—from about 20,000 per year to over 139,000 per year by 2004 (FIG. 1).[2]

[2] Fernandes, J. and Sorensen, R., "How Accreditation Enhances the MBA," AACSB 2005; US Department of Education, National Center for Education Statistics, Higher Education General Information Survey, 2005, Table 251; Ellin, A., "Was Earning That Harvard MBA Worth It?", *The New York Times*, June 11, 2006

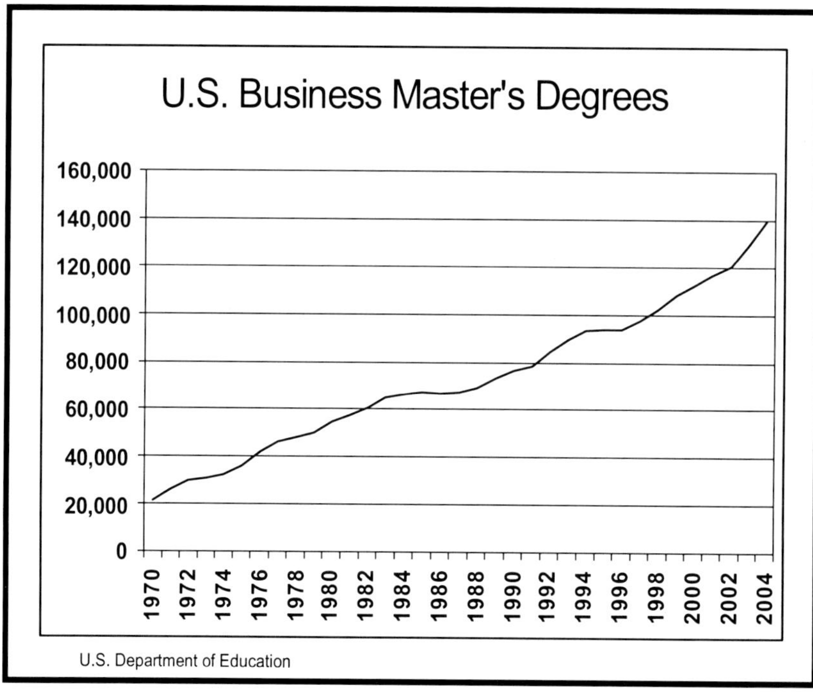

FIG. 1: GROWTH IN U.S. BUSINESS MASTER'S DEGREES AWARDED ANNUALLY

The primary reason for the continuing success of the MBA degree is the value it provides to those who earn it. A survey of 3,771 MBA graduates finds that eight years after graduation, 93% agree that their graduate management education was worth the time and investment.[3] Evidence from the 2005 *Forbes* survey of more than 6,000 business school alumni shows that graduates of

[3] "The GMAT Registrant Survey: Career and Educational Experiences," Graduate Management Admission Council, November 1999, pp. 3-6, A-6.

quality MBA programs achieve significant financial benefits.[4] For these alumni, it paid to get an MBA.

But statistics tell only part of the story. Ask the individual graduates how the MBA has changed their lives. For example, Steve, an engineer with a degree in optics, attended the part-time MBA program at the University of Rochester, where he was one of my students. After graduation, he worked for several small firms and then decided to start his own high-tech company in 2002. In 2004, sales were $1.6 million and in 2005 exceeded $4 million. His biggest challenge now is coping with the company's rapid growth. His future is very bright and he's using all of those management skills he learned in business school.

---

[4] Badenhausen, K. and Kump, L., "Best Business Schools," *Forbes*, September 5, 2005, p. 152.

2

TRENDS IN MBA APPLICATIONS

Applications to full-time MBA programs in the U.S. peaked in 2002, followed by a decline in 2003 and 2004, leading some in the media to speculate about whether the MBA degree was going out of style.

Such concerns about the future of the MBA are not new. Each decade brings fresh alarms.

- In the early 1970s, an article in *MBA Magazine* warned, "In the mid-1960s…the MBA could do no wrong...[but] by 1970, the once 'indispensable' MBA was being denounced as arrogant and overpaid. Many MBAs who had called their own tune as late as 1968 were, in 1970, out on the street looking for work."[5]
- In 1985, an article in *The Wall Street Journal* noted that "Some educators say that as many as 25 percent of the nation's 600 business schools may be forced to close

---

[5] Roscow, J., "Knocking Off the Golden Edge," *MBA Magazine*, August/September 1973, pp. 20-22.

because of the shrinking pool of applicants...after explosive growth in the 1970s, the number of MBA applicants is shrinking..."[6]

- Nearly a decade later, in 1993, *The New York Times* headlined, "Business Schools Hit Hard Times Amid Doubt Over Value of the MBA."[7] The number of prospective students taking the Graduate Management Admissions Test (GMAT) in late 1993 dropped 23 percent below the peak year of 1990.[8]
- In early 2005, *Business Week* reported, "...applications to Business Week's Top 30 MBA programs have dropped almost 30% overall since 1998, with some schools seeing declines of 50% or more."[9]

These variations in growth are due to short-term changes in economic and demographic conditions.[10] But as FIG. 1 shows, despite occasional flat spots, the number of degrees awarded has grown vigorously by a factor of nearly seven times since the early concerns in 1970, because earning an MBA has proven over time to be a valuable personal asset.

In the past few years, a number of articles have appeared asserting that the MBA degree has little value, that students who earn an MBA gain little in the way of salary increases or career choices, and that business schools need to completely overhaul

---

[6] Swartz, S., "Business Schools Revise Programs to Meet Firms' Changing Needs," *The Wall Street Journal*, March 28, 1985.
[7] Celis, W., "Business Schools Hit Hard Times Amid Doubt Over Value of the MBA," *The New York Times*, May 12, 1993, p. B6.
[8] Yeaple, R. N., "The MBA Advantage," Adams Publishing, 1994, p. 6.
[9] Merritt, J., "MBA Applicants are MIA," *Business Week*, April 18, 2005, pp. 28-30.
[10] "Application Trends Survey: 2005," Graduate Management Admission Council, 2005.

their course offerings.[11] Like the premature press reports about the demise of the MBA, these authors—some who are business school professors—are pessimistic about the future of the MBA degree and business schools in general.

In this book we will present compelling evidence that the critics are flat-out wrong, that there are substantial rewards—particularly financial rewards—for pursuing an MBA degree from a good school. It pays to get an MBA.

---

[11] See for example Pfeffer, J. and Fong, C., "The End of Business Schools? Less Success Than Meets the Eye," *Academy of Management Learning & Education*, Vol. 1, No. 1, September 2002, p. 3; and Mintzberg, H., "Managers Not MBAs," Berrett-Koehler Publishers, Inc., 2004.

3

REASONS FOR GETTING AN MBA DEGREE

There are many reasons for considering investing in an MBA degree:[12]

- Wider career choices. For most people, the MBA degree provides the qualifications and knowledge for moving up in their chosen field to a managerial position, or perhaps for changing fields altogether, such as from engineering to investment banking. A survey of MBA graduates showed that "interesting work" was most frequently mentioned as a "very important" reason for choosing the first job, outweighing the "compensation package."[13]
- Personal credentials. Having the letters "MBA" after your name signifies a commitment to professionalism in the

[12] Although some people may be uncomfortable with the idea of viewing education as an investment decision, the concept has a long and distinguished history. See, for example, Nobel Laureate Gary Becker's "Human Capital: A Theoretical and Empirical Analysis, with Special Reference to Education," National Bureau of Economic Research, Columbia University Press, 1964.

[13] "The GMAT Registrant Survey: Career and Educational Experiences," Graduate Management Admission Council, November 1999, p. 5-9.

field of management. You have paid your dues. This can be particularly important in large firms where credentials count. According to a study by McKinsey & Company, the percent of corporate CEOs with MBA degrees was 31% in 2000, up sharply from 23% a few years earlier.[14]

- A permanent asset. Unlike many other investments you might consider, the investment in an MBA results in a permanent personal asset. Jobs may come and go, but the MBA degree will stay with you throughout your professional career.
- Knowledge for its own sake. The MBA is a graduate degree. For most students, the coursework in an MBA program provides more than just a new set of managerial skills. It opens up a whole new way of making intelligent and informed decisions. You learn to be more objective and how to use data to illuminate complex choices. You project more confidence in your relations with others. When challenged in a meeting, you respond by saying, "I'm so glad you asked about this..." The knowledge gained will be of help not only in your job, but also in making important personal decisions such as buying a home or developing an investment portfolio.
- Make a contribution. Most of us want to make a contribution to the world around us, to make things better. How frustrating it is to work for a big company in a job that seems to have no impact. You go home at night knowing that the company will be successful—or unsuccessful—regardless of what you can do. You may dream that you want to become a leader in your

[14] McKinsey & Company, "Recent Trends in Business Education," January 2001.

profession, or perhaps you will want to start your own company some day. The MBA provides skills that can help make this dream possible.

- Study with bright professionals from around the world. In addition to what you will learn from your professors, you will learn much from your fellow students, who will have come from different professional backgrounds and in some cases, from different countries. By working in teams, you will learn how to provide leadership, and how to manage a project so that the goals are met on time and the results professionally presented to your peers. The sharing of experiences during classroom discussions and course projects is a major benefit of an MBA program.

- Networking. Your association with your business school and your fellow students will not end with graduation. You will become part of a network of highly motivated professionals who consider it a privilege to help each other throughout their careers.

- Financial gain. Pursing an MBA degree is a major investment decision. Even if financial gain is not your primary reason for getting an MBA, it's worth finding out whether the degree will pay for itself in a reasonably short time. Tuition may exceed $50,000, and if you go full-time, the opportunity cost of two years of foregone salary may add another $100,000 or more.

Does it pay to get an MBA degree? According to a recent survey of MBA graduates by *Forbes* magazine, on average those who graduate from a high quality AACSB-accredited MBA program see a substantial return on their investment within the first five years after graduation.[15]

Although each of these is a good reason for pursuing an MBA degree, the question of financial gain is one that is well suited for quantitative analysis and, in the case of the *Forbes* business school survey, as a basis for ranking MBA programs:

- It is an objective measure based on numbers, not subjective opinions or popularity contests.
- It is a market-based measure, based on what employers are willing to pay MBA graduates, not only at the time of graduation, but also during the first five years on the job.

[15] Badenhausen, K. and Kump, L., "Best Business Schools," *Forbes*, September 5, 2005, p. 152.

4

CONCERNS ABOUT THE VALUE OF THE MBA DEGREE

Despite the rapid growth in the number of MBA degrees awarded each year—and despite evidence that the MBA degree provides a high return on investment—in the past few years there have been a number of academic papers and magazine articles questioning the value of the MBA. The point of these articles is that individuals can be just as successful without an MBA. Moreover, the MBA provides no guarantee of success.

Certainly it is true that some individuals have achieved great success without an MBA, or without even an undergraduate degree. Consider Bill Gates, who dropped out of Harvard to found Microsoft, Steve Jobs, the inspirational leader of Apple Computer, or Michael Dell, who started Dell Computer. None of these has an MBA, or even a college degree. There are many other brilliant and highly motivated men and women who built successful companies or otherwise achieved great success without an MBA.

On the other side, there are those with MBA degrees who have been colossal failures. Jeff Skilling, former CEO of Enron Corporation and graduate of the Harvard Business School Class of 1979, was convicted in May 2006 of 19 counts of conspiracy, fraud, false statements, and insider trading for his role in the collapse of Enron. (His former boss at Enron, the late Ken Lay, held a Ph.D. in economics from the University of Houston and was also found guilty.)

Those who charge that the MBA degree does not *guarantee* success are quite correct. The question is whether it improves your chances for success—and whether it is worth the cost.

Some argue that the MBA, with its heavy emphasis on business analysis, is a detriment to creativity. As one wit put it, if Thomas Edison had had an MBA, instead of inventing the light bulb he would have developed a better pricing plan for candles.

Value added versus value multiplied

A number of years ago, the dean of a top business school was asked to explain the high starting salaries of the school's graduates. His response was, "We look for the best raw material we can find, filter it, put it in an expensive bottle with a fancy label, and sell it for a high price."

The dean's droll remark embodies the idea of "value added," that is, repackaging a product to add a fixed increment to its value. It's like saying that an MBA from Harvard is worth an additional $63,000 a year—the difference between Harvard's average pre-MBA salary of $85,000 and post-MBA starting pay of $143,000.[16]

---

[16] Post-MBA starting pay includes median salary, signing bonus, and other compensation. See "The Best B-Schools of 2004," *Business Week*, October 18, 2004, pp. 64-65.

Strictly speaking, the MBA does not add value, however, it *multiplies* it. Students with a great deal of talent and drive will get a lot more out of a degree from Harvard or Stanford than those with less ability and ambition.[17]

From a practical standpoint, what's the difference between value added and value multiplied? Consider the following example: Mike digs ditches for a living, and with a pick and shovel he can extend the length of the ditch at the rate of five feet per hour. Business is good, and Mike invests in a back hoe that allows him to dig at the rate of fifty feet per hour. The back hoe is a multiplier of Mike's ability to dig ditches. It multiplies his output by ten times.

Without Mike, the back hoe can't dig anything. It adds no fixed increment of value without an operator. Furthermore, in the hands of an inept or lazy operator, the back hoe might dig only ten feet per hour. The back hoe takes Mike's inherent talent and skill and multiplies it. That's what an MBA does, too.

Let's consider another example, one that involves education. John is a pharmaceutical salesman earning $50,000 per year calling on doctors. After three years in the field, John decides he would like to be a doctor himself. He quits his job, goes to medical school, and after eight years of education and training, he becomes a successful surgeon earning $200,000 per year.

For John, medical school is a value multiplier. His pay is four times as high as it was before, and he loves his work. Medical school does not add a fixed increment ($150,000) to John's pay that is independent of his talent. His success as a surgeon depends on his personal talent and skills. A classmate of his in medical

[17] This discussion is adapted from Yeaple, R. N., "The MBA Advantage," Adams Publishing, 1994, pp. 32-33.

school with less talent but going through the same educational process might not make it as a surgeon. The medical degree has no value without John. He can't sell it to someone else. The medical education *amplifies* John's personal abilities. It is a multiplier.

The MBA has no value by itself

Similarly, going to business school does not add value, it multiplies it. Students with drive and talent will get a lot more out of an MBA from a top business school than those with less ability. The MBA provides a set of fine tools for success. Some schools provide better tools than others. But success will come only if these tools are applied with skill and enthusiasm.

The value of a given school's MBA degree is therefore the product of its incoming student quality times the quality of its educational process.

{Value of MBA} = {Student quality} x {Educational process quality}

This means the value of a school's MBA degree is highly dependent on the quality of its incoming students. A business school may have an excellent faculty and top educational facilities, but if its incoming students are duds, its MBA degree will not be highly valued.[18] In this sense, the competitive game between the top schools is largely won or lost in the admissions office.

How do we know this is true? One measure of incoming student quality is the school's average GMAT score. As we will see in later chapters, the average economic value of a school's MBA degree is highly correlated with the average GMAT score of its incoming students (see, for example, FIG. 4).

---

[18] The economic value of a school's MBA is dependent on what employers are willing to pay its graduates.

In this sense, the dean who joked about the importance of starting with the best raw material had it exactly right.

Although incoming student quality is important in determining the economic value of a school's MBA degree, there are other factors at work that increase the value of a school's MBA. Some educational processes are more effective than others. In FIG. 5, for example, a number of schools are shown "above the line," which means they are providing additional value through their educational process beyond that which can be explained by student quality alone.

Most likely this is the result of superior teaching. (If all schools provided exactly the same quality of educational process and the only thing that mattered was incoming student quality, all the data points in FIGS. 4 and 5 would lie right along the trend line and the R^2 would equal 1.00.)

Taking on the critics

This explanation—that an MBA degree provides a set of fine tools—sets the stage for an analysis of the arguments of those who criticize the value of the MBA. Some will point out that the MBA is no guarantee of success—that many who earn the MBA are not successful. Others note that Bill Gates and others did well without an MBA.

Much of the criticism of the value of MBA programs comes from those who teach in top business schools. In a 1980 *Harvard Business School* article, "Managing Our Way to Economic Decline," a pair of Harvard Business School professors took their business school colleagues to task for "a preference for analytical detachment rather than the insight that comes from hands-on experience."[19] Somehow the economy managed to avoid declining in the decades that followed.

In 2002, a Stanford Business School professor, Jeffrey Pfeffer and his graduate student, Christina Fong, created a sensation in the popular press when they reported:

> "There is little evidence that mastery of the knowledge acquired in business schools enhances people's careers, or that even attaining the MBA credential itself has much effect on graduates' salaries or career attainment."[20]

This is a remarkable statement, given the overwhelming evidence that for leading business schools, post-MBA starting pay jumps 50% to 100% or more above pre-MBA pay and continues on an accelerated path in the years immediately following graduation.[21] At Stanford (Pfeffer's school) median post-MBA starting pay is reported to be $150,000, compared to pre-MBA pay of $75,000.[22]

There are many reasons for earning an MBA besides financial gain. But while there certainly is room for constructive debate on how to improve the quality of MBA programs, Pfeffer and Fong's central assertion in their paper—that a degree from a leading school provides little or no value—disqualifies it from serious consideration.

Another business school professor, Henry Mintzberg of McGill University in Montreal, authored a 2004 book, "Managers

---

[19] Hayes, R. and Abernathy, W., "Managing Our Way to Economic Decline," *Harvard Business Review*, July-August 1980.

[20] Pfeffer, J. and Fong, C., "The End of Business Schools? Less Success Than Meets the Eye," *Academy of Management Learning & Education*, Vol. 1, No. 1, September 2002, p. 3.

[21] "The Top Business Schools," Forbes, September 5, 2005, p. 152; "The Best B-Schools of 2004," *Business Week*, October 18, 2004, pp. 64-65.

[22] "The Best B-Schools of 2004," *Business Week*, October 18, 2004, pp. 64-65;

Not MBAs," in which he reviews the history of business schools and found much that he said needs improving in today's MBA programs.[23] He advocates that the best time to provide full-time education for managers is in mid-career after they have had some business experience, not in their early- or mid-twenties as in traditional full-time MBA programs.

While the argument has some merit given the success of part-time executive MBA programs for mid-career managers, asking fast-trackers to drop out of the work force in mid-career to attend a *full-time* MBA program ignores the huge opportunity cost in terms of lost salary and lost career momentum these students would incur.

As we shall see in the next chapter, to properly evaluate the value of a full-time MBA program, the opportunity costs of being out of the workforce must be included.

Yet Mintzberg persists. Interviewed for a *New York Times* article in June 2006, he said:

> "MBA programs train the wrong people in the wrong ways with the wrong consequences."[24]

But like Pfeffer, Mintzberg is unable to explain why employers continue to pay such high post-MBA starting salaries. The thousands of employers who hire MBAs each year are clearly able to determine whether the premium starting salaries and bonuses they pay are worth it. If the MBA degree truly adds little value, as Pfeffer and Mintzberg assert, companies would soon learn to hire right out of undergraduate programs at half the salaries they pay MBAs.

---

[23] Mintzberg, H., "Managers Not MBAs," Berrett-Koehler Publishers, Inc., 2004.

[24] Ellin, A., "Was Earning That Harvard MBA Worth It?", *The New York Times*, June 11, 2006.

Ever since introducing the first business school ranking in 1988, *Business Week* magazine has been a strong advocate of the value of the MBA degree.[25] But in a recent *Business Week* article, "Is the MBA Overrated?", writer Louis Lavelle raised a new concern. In a new survey he found that most of the top executives of the Standard & Poor's Top 100 companies made it to the top without an MBA.

> "*Business Week* examined the five highest-paid executives at each of the S&P 100 companies…Only 146 of the 500 executives reported having MBAs.."[26]

But a much earlier *Business Week* survey (1990) found that in the case of Harvard at least, the great majority of Harvard MBAs chose not to work for very large corporations. According to an article that appeared in the June 18, 1990 issue of *Business Week*, a survey of the Harvard Business School class of 1970 found that only 13 percent worked for Top 1000 firms and only four of the 723 alumni were CEOs of Top 1000 firms. The great majority were entrepreneurs or managers in small companies.

The reason that many of the graduates of MBA programs are not CEOs of major corporations may be that they have found that being an entrepreneur or running a small business is financially more rewarding, less subject to public criticism, and more fun.

In summary, MBA education will continue to face criticism and much of it will be constructive. In today's fast changing business environment, business schools will be challenged to keep up.

But it is important to keep in mind that employers are paying record salaries and bonuses for graduates of the leading business

---

[25] See, for example, Merritt, J., "What's an MBA Really Worth," *Business Week*, September 22, 2003.

[26] Lavelle, L., "Is the MBA Overrated?", *Business Week*, March 20, 2006.

schools. These companies would not hire MBAs year after year at these high salaries unless they believe they are getting good value for their money. The economic value of the MBA is not based on what the critics say—it is based on what employers are willing to pay.

In the following chapter, a method for calculating the value of an MBA degree will be presented.

5

"THE MBA ADVANTAGE" FINANCIAL GAIN MODEL

"The MBA Advantage" financial gain model was developed when Judith, a prospective student, asked the following question: "How much more money will I have five years after graduation, versus staying in my old job without an MBA degree?"

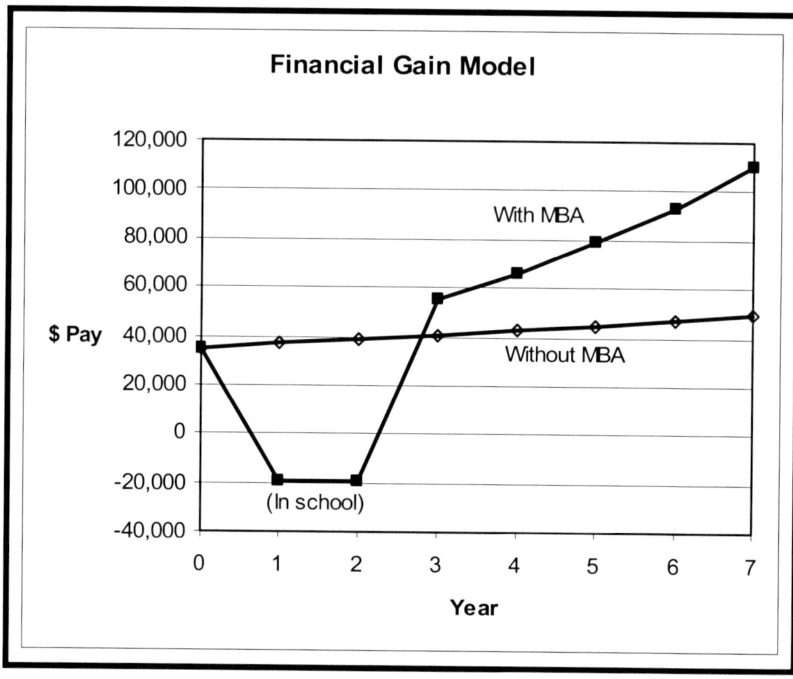

FIG. 2: "THE MBA ADVANTAGE" FINANCIAL GAIN MODEL[27]

At the left of this graph (FIG. 2) is Judith's current salary of $35,000 per year. She is weighing the decision of whether or not to pursue a full-time MBA degree.

---

[27] This financial gain model was first developed in Yeaple, R.N., "The MBA Advantage," Adams Publishing, 1994. It has since been adopted with modifications by *Forbes* magazine for its biennial survey of leading business schools.

- If she chooses to stay in her current job and not pursue the MBA, she estimates she can expect an annual salary increase of 5% per year, and 7 years from now she will be making about $49,000 per year (open dots).
- On the other hand, if she enrolls in a full-time MBA program with tuition of $20,000 per year (solid dots), based on the success of other graduates in this program she expects a post-MBA starting salary of about $55,000 in year 3, and a salary by year 7 of about $110,000.
- The financial gain from the MBA is then the cumulative difference between the two curves, which in this example is about $60,000.

This example shows that 5 years after graduating with her MBA, Judith expects to have recovered all the costs of earning the MBA, including the tuition and the foregone salary, and will be ahead by about $60,000.[28] Although the analysis in this model cuts off at the end of 5 years post-MBA, the financial gains from the MBA will continue to accrue for the rest of her professional career, and could amount to many hundreds of thousands of dollars.

As we saw in the previous chapter, the value of a given business school's MBA degree is dependent on the quality of its incoming students. The curves in FIG. 2 represent the average gain for that school. But if Judith is more talented and ambitious than her classmates, her gain at the end of 5 years post-MBA will exceed the $60,000 average for her school. If on the other hand she is less motivated, she might not do as well.

---

[28] This example uses numbers from a survey of students taken some years ago at a leading business school. For more details, see Yeaple, R.N., "The Success Principle," Macmillian, 1997, pp. 71-76. While the numbers will be different for various individuals, they are typical for many of the leading schools surveyed in the *Forbes* 2005 business school survey.

Therefore, when we talk about the financial gain for an MBA from a given school, it is important to recognize that this is for the average student graduating from that school. Some of that school's graduates will do better; some will not do as well.

Putting it another way, the value you can expect from a school's MBA is highly dependent on how much effort you are willing to put into your coursework and your subsequent job search.

With nearly 140,000 master's degrees in business now being awarded annually (FIG. 1), there may be close to 300,000 individuals pursuing an MBA degree in the U.S. at any point in time, given that it typically takes two or more years to complete the degree. (A small proportion may be pursuing one-year MS degrees.)

Although the traditional two-year full-time MBA program is most often mentioned in articles about the value of the MBA degree, in fact the great majority of MBA students are part-timers.

> "[About] 20% of business school students are enrolled in [traditional] two-year, full-time programs. Part-time evening and weekend programs account for half of current students; the rest are enrolled in executive, distance-learning and other smaller programs."[29]

Some experts report that part-time and executive programs are showing the most growth:

> " 'Part-time programs are the staple now,' says John Fernandes, president of the Association to Advance Collegiate Schools of Business, the MBA accrediting group. 'Growth in these programs is reflective of society at large. Everyone is

---

[29] Badenhausen, K. and Kump, L., "Best Business Schools," *Forbes*, September 5, 2005, p. 148.

too busy to stop their careers and go through a concentrated two-year program.' "[30]

But others are convinced that the total immersion 24/7 of a full-time program is clearly superior because it avoids the distraction of trying to hold a job while going to school. For career changers and for students with little or no pre-MBA work experience, the full-time program may be the better choice.

"MBA Lite—that's what many corporate recruiters call the various alternatives to a full-time program."[31]

As we shall see in the next sections, each kind of MBA program—full-time, part-time (including executive) and online—has its advantages and disadvantages. The choice depends on the individual student's circumstances and on his or her goals in pursuing an MBA.

---

[30] Ibid.

[31] Alsop, R., "The Full-Time Advantage," *The Wall Street Journal*, September 21, 2005, p. R4.

PART II

THE FULL-TIME MBA

6

THE VALUE OF A FULL-TIME MBA PROGRAM

Continuing with our earlier example, a full-time MBA program requires going without salary during the two years in school (see FIG. 3). During these two years, Judith's cash flow is negative. The opportunity cost of these two years of foregone salary must be included along with the tuition in calculating the total investment in the degree program.

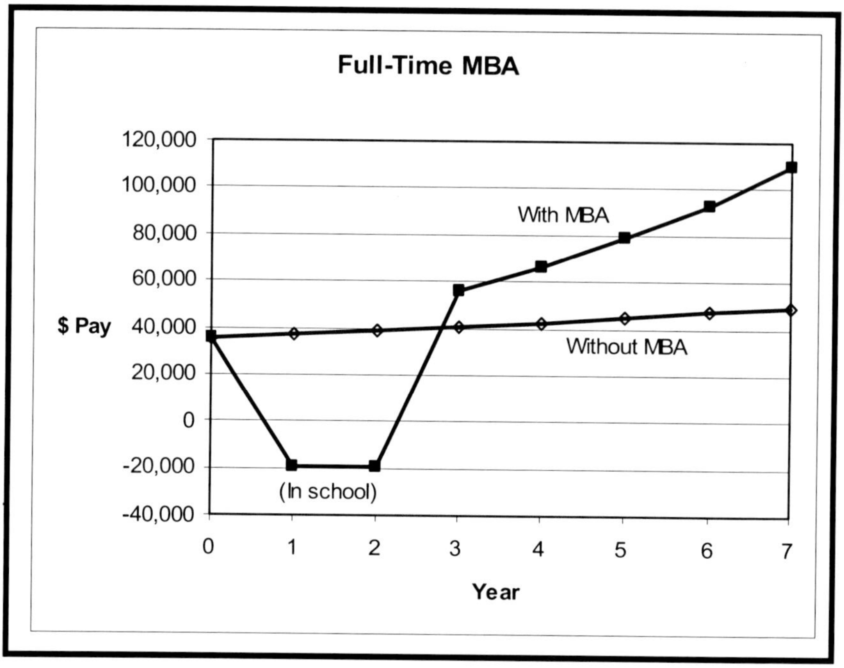

FIG. 3: FINANCIAL GAIN MODEL FOR A FULL-TIME MBA PROGRAM

The additional investment of two years of foregone salary makes the full-time program the most expensive option for pursing an MBA. Nevertheless, data from the *Forbes* 2005 survey of top business schools shows that the full-time degree can more than pay for itself in the first five years following graduation.

By plotting the *Forbes* data in FIG. 4 we see that the post-MBA five-year gain for leading business schools ranges from just a few thousand dollars to nearly $140,000 for the top-ranked school.

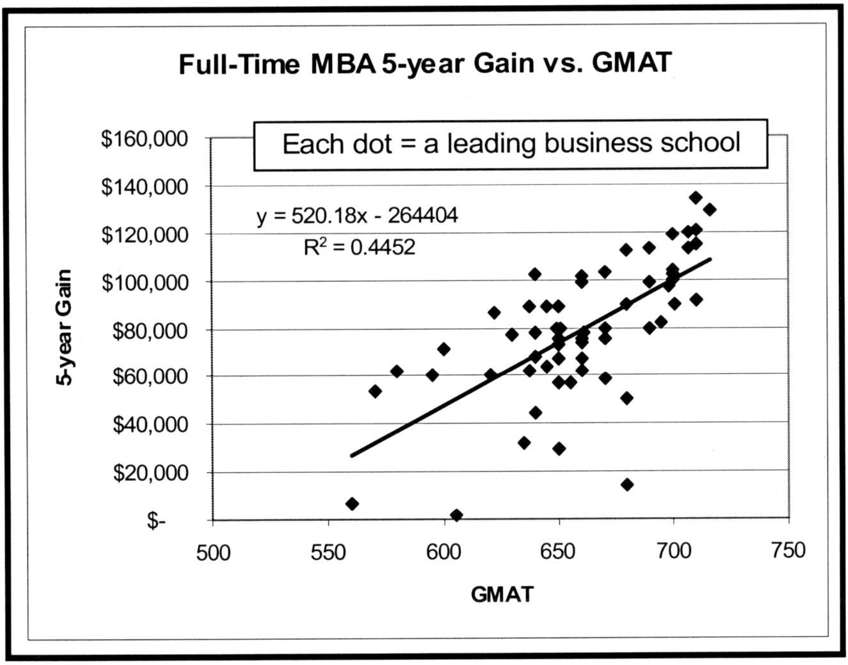

FIG. 4: *FORBES* SURVEY DATA ON FIVE-YEAR GAIN FOR FULL-TIME MBA PROGRAMS

Note that the trend line indicates that in general the higher a school's average GMAT score, the higher that school's five-year gain.[32] A separate study by the Graduate Management Admission

[32] The trend line was calculated by ordinary least squares regression analysis. The R^2 of 0.4452 means that about 45% of the variation in five-year gain across these schools can be explained by the variation in average GMAT scores.

Council confirms this association. Students graduating from schools requiring GMATs of 650 or higher had significantly higher starting salaries and continued to have higher salaries eight years after graduation, compared to those from schools accepting GMATs lower than 650.[33]

Our financial gain model (FIG. 4) shows that after paying the costs of a full-time MBA from a top school (including the opportunity cost of foregone salary), the average student will have a gain ranging from a few thousand dollars to as much as $140,000 five years after graduating. The average five-year gain for the 60 leading schools shown in FIG. 4 is $78,833.

But what about gains from an MBA that is not from a top school? In a study prepared for the U.S. House of Representatives, economists Antony Davies and Thomas Cline addressed this question:

> "This analysis...simply attempts to show whether or not average, plain-vanilla MBAs can expect to fare better or worse that average college graduates over the entire course of their careers."[34]

Using data from the Statistical Abstracts of the United States and from the Graduate Management Admission Council, Davies and Cline concluded that in constant 2003 dollars, the net present value of a "plain-vanilla" MBA over the course of one's entire career exceeds $500,000:

> "Clearly, not all MBAs attain greater compensation and career benefits than their counterparts with bachelor's degrees. Still, it's even clearer that the 'average' MBA

---

[33] "The GMAT Registrant Survey: Career and Educational Experiences," Graduate Management Admission Council, November 1999, pp. 5-8, 6-6, 5-7.
[34] Davies, A. and Cline, T., "The ROI on the MBA," *BizEd*, January/February 2005, pp. 42-45.

> fares spectacularly better than the 'average' college graduate. Getting a plain-vanilla MBA is like receiving a tax-free cash award of more than a half-million dollars."[35]

The number from the Davies and Cline study—more than a $500,000 gain from an "average" MBA over one's entire career—is consistent with an average gain of $78,800 from a top school over the first five years of one's career. This provides a "reasonableness confirmation" of the data shown in FIG. 4. Davies and Cline based their study on data from the Statistical Abstracts of the United States and the Graduate Management Admission Council. The data in FIG. 4 are from an entirely different source—a 2005 survey of MBA graduates by *Forbes* magazine.

This consistency between the two studies provides confidence that the results are representative of the value of the MBA degree, and that the critics who claim the MBA has no value are simply wrong.

[35] Ibid., p. 45.

7

THE *FORBES* MODEL PROVIDES A CONSERVATIVE VALUE FOR THE FULL-TIME MBA

The financial gain model used by *Forbes* offers a valuable method for comparing business schools. The methodology for the 2005 *Forbes* business school survey is described in Appendix A. *Forbes* provides a convenient online calculator on its website that prospective students can use to calculate their own expected five-year gain at various leading schools by entering their personal data on pre-MBA pay, etc. It may be accessed at:

http://www.forbes.com/2005/08/16/cz_05mba_business_schools_gain_calulator.html

While the *Forbes* online calculator is fast and easy to use, it may tend to understate the true value of a full-time MBA for many students:

- The model cuts off at the end of five years post-MBA (FIG. 3). As noted previously, the value of the degree continues to accrue over the individual's professional lifetime.

- According to the U.S Department of Education, 61 percent of full-time MBA students hold outside jobs, working an average of 34 hours per week. The assumption used in the *Forbes* model—spending two years in school without any income whatsoever—may overstate the opportunity cost of two years of foregone salary for many students.[36]
- The *Forbes* model uses each school's published "sticker price" for tuition. Most schools offer scholarships (discounts from the sticker price) for good students, ranging all the way up to full tuition, so the model may overstate the true cost of tuition.

Therefore, the financial gains for full-time MBA programs plotted in FIG. 4 should be considered as conservative. For full-time students who work part-time and for those who earn scholarships, the real financial gains from earning a full-time MBA should be higher.

A more flexible version of the full-time five-year financial gain model that avoids some of these limitations is provided as an Excel spreadsheet in Appendix B. Using this spreadsheet you can estimate the five-year financial gain from a full-time MBA by entering each of the following variables as assumptions:

Pre-MBA pay (e.g., $35,000)

Growth rate without an MBA (e.g., 5%)

Tuition /year, less scholarships (e.g., $20,000)

Post-MBA starting salary (e.g., $60,000)

Signing bonus (e.g., $10,000)

---

[36] "Percent of graduate and first-professional students who worked while enrolled," U.S. Department of Education, National Center for Educational Statistics, 1999-2000 National Postsecondary Student Aid Study (NPSAS: 2000).

Post-MBA growth rate (e.g., 15%)

Discount rate (e.g., 4%)

The model will then calculate the five-year gain.

8

SPECIAL ADVANTAGES OF THE FULL-TIME DEGREE

The full-time program, while initially more costly than other options, offers special advantages not found in other choices:

- Career changers: For those students planning a major career change, such as David's desire to switch from engineering to investment banking, the 24/7 total immersion of a full-time program provides maximum exposure to the skills and knowledge required for success in the new field.
- Summer internship: The internship offered between the first and second year of a full-time program is an excellent way for David to become acquainted with a new employer. Many top companies find that the summer internship is the most effective way to recruit MBAs for permanent employment after graduation.
- Extra help for students with little or no work experience: David entered business school with no work experience, and he will gain from the total immersion of the full-time program. For students like David, having a summer internship is critical for landing a good job upon graduation.

- Job interviews: All leading business schools offer extensive Career Management services to assist students in finding summer internships and permanent employment. But to maximize the value of these services, David must be on campus during the day to meet with potential employers.

For students considering a major career change, or for those with little or no pre-MBA work experience, the full-time option may be the best choice.

9

ADDED VALUE FROM SCHOOLS WITH GREAT TEACHING

In FIG. 4, some schools were shown above the line, while others were below the line. If a school is above the line, this suggests that the school is providing extra value to its students beyond that which can be explained by GMAT scores alone.[37] Most likely, this is the result of superior teaching. Two such "above the line" business schools, Rollins and Dartmouth, are highlighted in FIG. 5.

[37] Statisticians will recognize this as a positive residual.

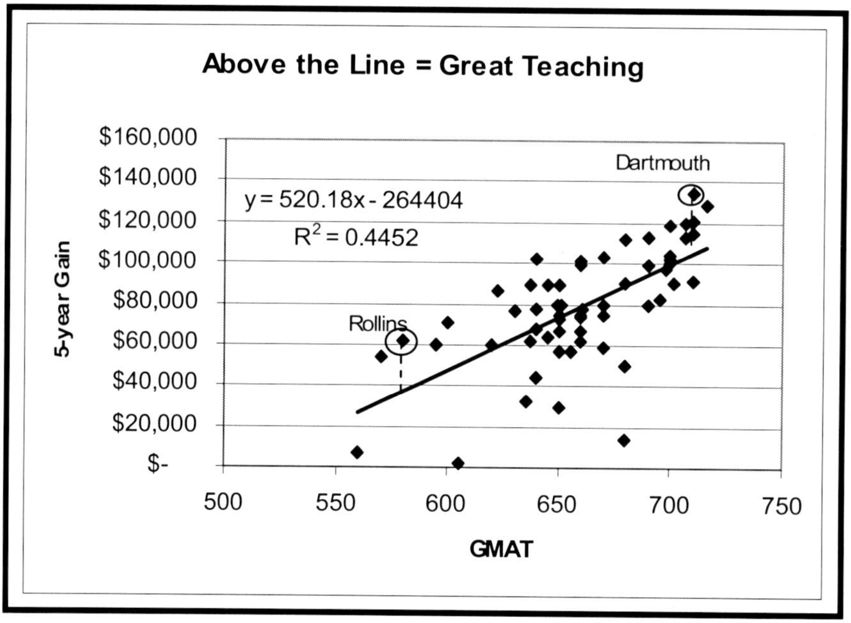

FIG. 5: "ABOVE THE LINE" SUGGESTS ADDED VALUE FOR STUDENTS FROM SUPERIOR TEACHING.

Good teaching has not always been a priority at many of the leading business schools. Before *Business Week* began ranking MBA programs in 1988, faculty hiring and promotion decisions were based almost entirely on research productivity—the number of scholarly papers a faculty member published in the top research journals. Young faculty members seeking tenure were cautioned to "not over-invest in teaching"—in other words, to concentrate on research. Consequently, some of the business school teaching in those days was abysmal.

The rankings changed all that. Once schools learned that student satisfaction—one of the two major components in the

Business Week ranking—had a big effect on applications, teaching quality became very important. Young untenured faculty were now told that student evaluations of their teaching would have a significant bearing on promotion and tenure decisions—but research productivity would still dominate.

Many young faculty found this change in the rules of the game to be extremely stressful. Senior faculty worried that courses were being dumbed down and grades inflated to keep students happy, at the expense of real learning in challenging courses. The implication was that students preferred easy courses with little challenge instead of demanding learning experiences, even though they were paying $100,000 or more for their education.

Time will tell whether the learning experience of the MBA has been diluted. If graduates are hired and found to have fewer skills than in the past, companies will reduce their hiring of MBAs and will pay less for those they do hire.

On the other hand, companies will pay a premium for students from those schools that excel in educating their graduates with the knowledge and skills necessary for managerial success.

The premium employers are willing to pay for graduates from schools that do a superior job of teaching may already be showing up as above-the-line values in the *Forbes* financial gain data. Note, for example, that Rollins College is above the line in both FIG. 5 (full-time programs) and FIG. 6 (part-time programs), suggesting this is a real premium for good teaching and not just a random positive residual due to chance. (There were about 6,000 respondents to the 2005 *Forbes* survey and 60 full-time programs are shown in FIG. 5, so on average each data point shown represents the median of about 100 responses from each school's alumni.)

10

IS PRE-MBA WORK EXPERIENCE NECESSARY?

Anne is about to graduate from a liberal arts college and has no pre-MBA work experience. Should she apply now for admission to business school, or should she work for a few years before applying?

Many business schools expect their applicants to have pre-MBA work experience of 3 to 5 years. Moreover, the amount of desired work experience has increased in recent years. In the 1960s and 1970s, most students pursued their MBA right after their undergraduate program. In the 1980s, employers began to express a preference for MBAs with some work experience. Ten years ago, the average age of a first-year MBA was 25 years old. Today it is 28.[38]

Arguments in favor of pre-MBA work experience are:

- Students with work experience are more sensitive to the problems of managing a business and have insights into what is being presented in class.
- Having students with work experience in the classroom contributes to a richer discussion of business problems and opportunities.
- Work experience gives employers more information on which to evaluate prospective hires for evidence of leadership and other personal skills.

But for some full-time students, the benefits of 3 to 5 years of pre-MBA work experience may not be justified by the costs:

- There is an increasing awareness that dropping out of the workforce at age 28 for two years creates a large opportunity cost, not only in terms of foregone salary but also in terms of lost career momentum, particularly in fast-moving high-tech industries. For most individuals, the opportunity cost is much lower immediately following graduation from an undergraduate program.
- A recent survey (2004) found that those MBA students with more work experience did not graduate with significantly higher grades or greater starting salaries, nor did they report much higher job satisfaction after graduation.[39]

---

[38] "Work Experience," mba.com, Graduate Management Admission Council.
[39] Dreher, G. and Ryan, K., "A Suspect MBA Selection Model: The Case Against the Standard Work-Experience Requirement," *Academy of Management Learning and Education*, 2004, **3** , pp. 87-91.

- An earlier study (1997) showed that by age 30 there was no significant correlation between pay and pre-MBA work experience. The amount of pre-MBA work experience appeared to have no significant effect on long-term pay.[40]
- At the University of Rochester, where students with no work experience account for nearly 20% of the enrollment, Dean Mark Zupan says that "... young students...are outperforming (older students) in terms of job offers."[41]
- At Rollins College, younger students have been found to be easier to place in post-MBA jobs. They are more flexible about moving because they are less likely to have families. They are more eager to accept their first job and are less likely to leave the company in the first few years. And they are easier to place because without work experience, their initial post-MBA salaries are lower (although as noted above, by age 30 they tend to be paid about the same as those who wait to get work experience before starting their MBA).
- Business schools are anxious to increase the proportion of women enrolled in MBA programs from the current 35%. Many women are reluctant to wait until age 27 or 28 before entering business school because they would like to use this time in their lives to start a family. According to *U.S. News & World Report*, some schools are reducing the work

[40] A 1995 survey of 273 Simon School MBA graduates from the University of Rochester found that pre-MBA work experience had a significant positive effect on starting pay ($t = 2.843$, $p = 0.0057$), but it appeared to have no measurable effect on long-term pay ($t = 0.19$, $p = 0.8496$). See Yeaple, R.N., "The Success Principle," Macmillan, 1997, pp. 244-245.

[41] Gloeckler, G., "Who Needs the Real World?" *Business Week*, February 13, 2006.

experience requirement for women so that they can enter at an earlier age.[42]

- Two top business schools, Harvard and Stanford, now accept some MBA students with little or no work experience.
- Finally, the 2005 *Forbes* survey shows that the five-year gain for a school such as Rollins, which accepts a significant proportion of its full-time students with little or no work experience, is comparable to that of other leading schools that require more work experience. The five-year gain for Rollins is $62,000, compared with an average of $78,800 for the 60 top schools in the *Forbes* survey.

Most leading schools still prefer their applicants to have significant work experience. But prospective students without work experience who are bright and articulate and have demonstrated leadership in their undergraduate program may find that they are welcomed at leading business schools. As the Harvard Business School website states:

> "There is no minimum age or work experience required to apply to HBS…Pursuing an MBA early in your career can increase the long-term possibility for personal, professional, and financial growth."

Similarly, the Stanford website encourages younger students to apply:

> "If you are ready to accelerate your leadership development, don't wait. Start now…. We don't require a minimum level of work experience."

[42] Ramachandran, N., "Looking for Ms. MBA," *U.S. News & World Report*, America's Best Graduate Schools, 2007 edition, p. 9

Anne, who has no work experience, should go online and search for those leading schools that will accept students without work experience. Some schools are willing to accept women with little or no work experience in order to increase the proportion of women in their programs. She might find that she can get an early start on the higher salary and increased job satisfaction that come with earning an MBA.

11

FINANCING A FULL-TIME MBA DEGREE

A full-time program requires a significant front-end investment (tuition plus two years of foregone salary, as shown in FIG. 3). For many students this may require taking out a loan. Because the federal government considers investment in higher education to be in the public interest, it has created the Federal Stafford Loan Program.

- Subsidized Stafford loans, up to a maximum of $8,500 per year, are need-based. The federal government pays the interest on these loans while the student is in school and during a six-month grace period after the student leaves school. Repayment begins six months after leaving school and extends up to ten years.

- Unsubsidized Stafford loans, up to a maximum of $18,500 per year, are not need-based and are available to graduate students living independent of their parents. The borrower is responsible for the interest on the loan as soon as it is taken out. Similar to subsidized loans, repayment begins six months after leaving school and extends up to ten years.

In 1999-2000, 44 percent of full-time MBA students took out Stafford Loans for an average amount of $14,616.[43] For more on the Stafford Loan Program, visit the program's official website at:

www.salliemae.com/apply/borrowing/stafford.html.

---

43 "Percentage of graduate and first-professional students with Stafford loans," U.S. Department of Education, National Center for Educational Statistics, 1999-2000 National Postsecondary Student Aid Study (NPSAS: 2000).

PART III

THE PART-TIME AND EXECUTIVE MBA

12

ADVANTAGES OF PART-TIME AND EXECUTIVE MBA PROGRAMS

Michael has a family and a job with a company that is growing fast and has good long-term potential. His motivation for getting an MBA is to move up as a manager in his company. Leaving his job for two years to attend a full-time program is not an acceptable option.

For many prospective MBA students with family obligations or who have jobs they enjoy, going to business school full-time is not a practical option. For these students, does it pay to get a part-time MBA?

According to the *Forbes* 2005 survey, a part-time degree from a leading business school also provides a positive return on investment (see FIG. 6). Note again that some schools, notably Rollins and NYU, are "above the line," suggesting superior teaching.

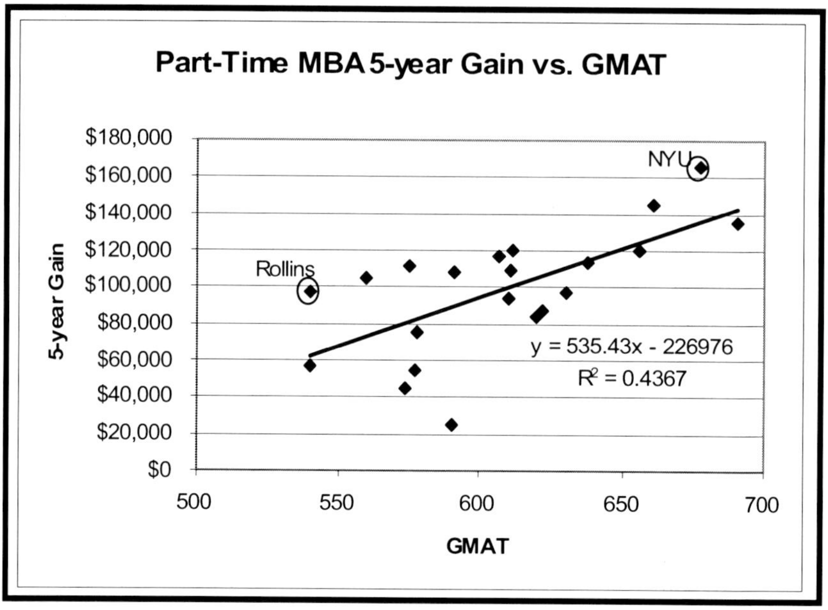

FIG. 6: *FORBES* SURVEY DATA ON FIVE-YEAR GAIN FOR PART-TIME MBA PROGRAMS

Part-time programs and executive programs have a number of advantages:

- Since most people who take part-time programs do so at a local business school, there's no need to move. You avoid the cost and disruption of living somewhere else for two years.
- You continue to make a salary while you are in school. The biggest cost of a full-time MBA is not the tuition; it's the salary you give up for the two years you are in school.

- You continue to be employed when you graduate. If you plan to change employers after getting a part-time MBA, the job change can take place at *your* convenience.
- Students in part-time and executive programs tend to be older and more experienced than those in full-time programs. Much of the richness of what you learn in business school is the result of classroom discussions with your fellow students who come from different professional backgrounds and, in some cases, from other countries.
- For many part-time MBA students, employers will pick up part of the tuition.

For Michael, with family obligations and a job he enjoys, a part-time or executive MBA program at a quality business school is the right choice.

13

PART-TIME PROGRAMS GENERALLY PROVIDE HIGHER FINANCIAL GAINS

One of the most interesting results from the *Forbes* 2005 survey is the finding that a student's financial gain from a school's part-time MBA program usually exceeds that from the same school's full-time MBA.

In FIG. 7, for the 20 business schools that display both part-time gains (dark bars) and full-time gains (light bars), 17 (85%) show that the part-time gain is higher.[44]

---

[44] The data for FIG. 7 is for traditional part-time programs and does not include executive programs.

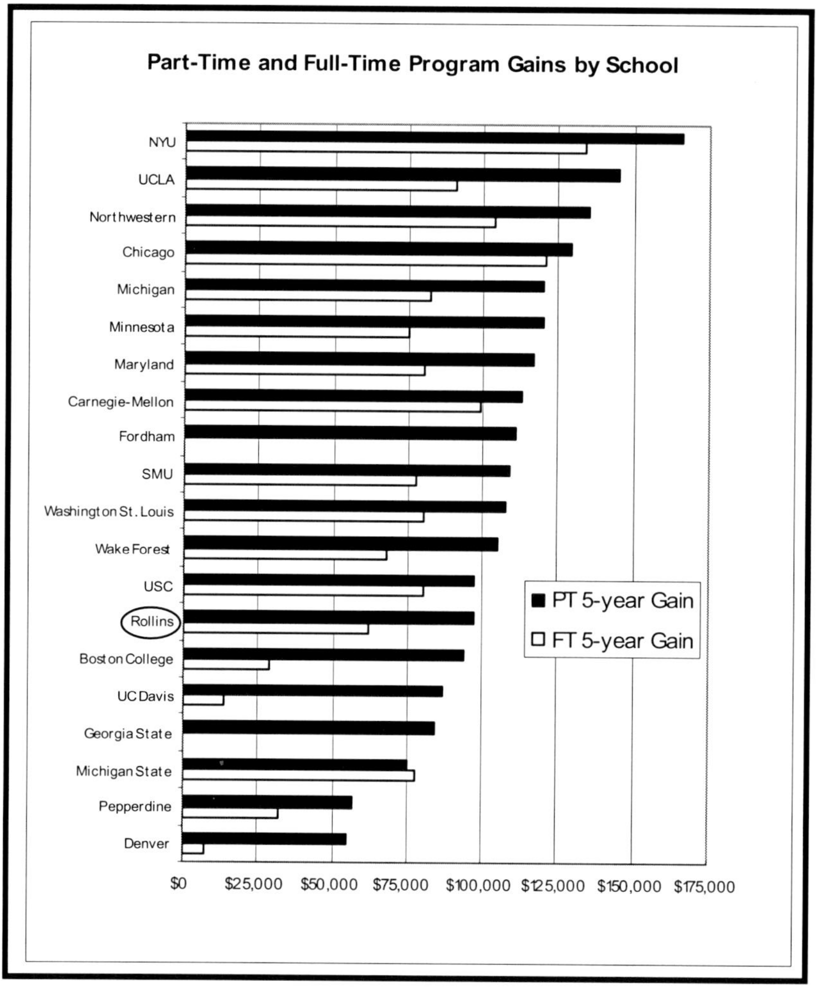

FIG. 7: PART-TIME AND FULL-TIME MBA PROGRAM GAINS BY SCHOOL

The reason is that for the same benefit, the part-time program requires less investment—there is no opportunity cost of foregone salary, which is typically the largest cost of a full-time program. For most schools, the quality of teaching in the part-time program is the same as in the full-time program. So while the benefit may be the same, the cost of the part-time program is less, and the return on investment is higher.

This does not mean that a part-time program is the better choice for everyone. Students without pre-MBA work experience and those considering a major career change may find that the full-time program is the preferred option.

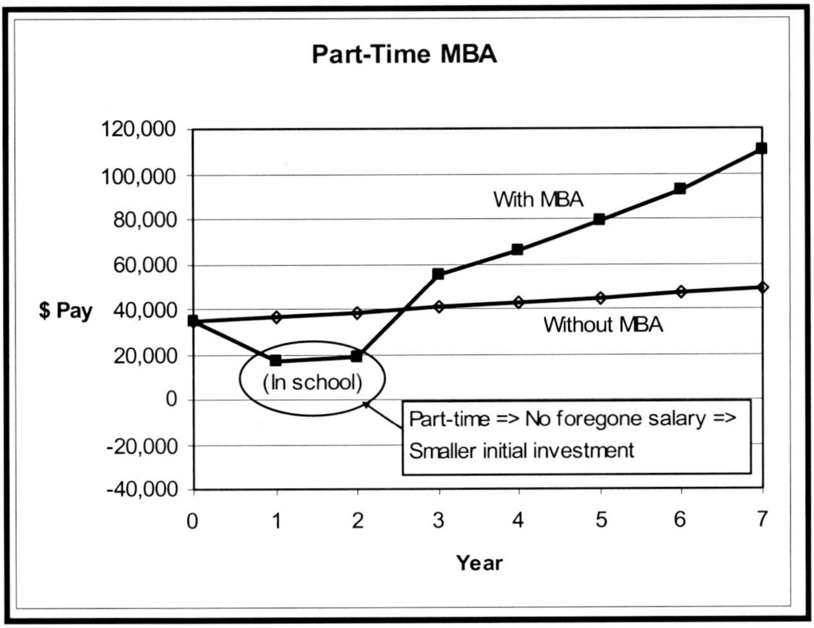

FIG. 8: FINANCIAL GAIN MODEL FOR A PART-TIME MBA PROGRAM

The lower investment required in a part-time program is shown graphically in FIG. 8. A comparison of the investment in the part-time program is less than for the full-time program shown in FIG. 3, so the financial gain is higher.

An Excel spreadsheet for part-time programs that you can customize for your situation is provided in Appendix C.

14

ADVANTAGES OF AN ONLINE MBA PROGRAM

Online MBA programs are reported to be expanding rapidly. The University of Phoenix is a major supplier of online MBA programs.

> "With yearly enrollment numbering about 16,000, the University of Phoenix online MBA program…reports year-to-year growth in excess of 50% since its inception in 1989."[45]

For students with a heavy travel schedule or a work schedule that does not permit attending classes at night or on weekends, an online program may be the only option for earning an MBA degree.

---

[45] Gangemi, J., "Do Online MBAs Make the Grade?" *Business Week Online*, August 18, 2005.

However, most online programs (including the University of Phoenix) are not accredited by the AACSB, the premier accrediting organization for business schools. Some are low quality diploma mills. *Business Week* reports that recruiters are wary of online degrees:

> "For those who expect the same respect from corporate recruiters, think again. 'The only way we'd hire [an MBA with an online degree] is if their résumé is strong and they can explain why they had to get their MBA online,' says Gloria Odogbili, assistant MBA recruiter for UBS Investment Bank in New York."[46]

A recent survey of corporate recruiters by *The Wall Street Journal* found that "About 80% of recruiters said these (online) programs are not as effective in developing skills as a full-time MBA." One respondent to the survey noted that what's missing from online programs is the valuable student interaction. She stated that she often learned the most as an MBA student from fellow students who brought abstract business problems to life for her.[47]

Students looking for an online MBA program should consider only those of the highest quality, such as the University of Indiana's Kelley Direct online program, which is fully accredited by the AACSB. The faculty of the Kelley Direct program all teach in the school's highly-regarded full-time and part-time MBA programs as well.

---

[46] Gangemi, J., "Do Online MBAs Make the Grade?" *Business Week Online*, August 18, 2005.

[47] Alsop, R., "The Full-Time Advantage," *The Wall Street Journal*, September 21, 2005, p. R4.

PART IV

CHOOSING A BUSINESS SCHOOL

15

THE RANKING GAME

We love to have things ranked. J.D. Power ranks automobiles. *Consumer Reports* ranks cameras and dishwashers. *Business Week*, *U.S. News & World Report*, *The Wall Street Journal*, and *Forbes* all rank business schools.[48]

These rankings can be helpful. Buying cameras and cars—and MBA degrees—are difficult and complex purchase decisions. As consumers we often have little or no prior experience in buying some of these expensive products. This is particularly true of MBA degrees since people buy only one in their lifetime and we can't draw on our experience when choosing an MBA program. We need expert advice.

Which schools are the best business schools? This is an important question to potential students who are about to invest $150,000 or more (including the opportunity cost of two years of

[48] Parts of this section are adapted from Yeaple, R.N., "The MBA Advantage," Adams Publishing, 1994, chapter 3.

foregone salary). Even among the leading schools, the choice of business school can make a huge difference, as much as $140,000 in financial return within the first five years of graduation (see FIG. 4.)

In this chapter we will evaluate four different ways to rank business schools:

- The biennial *Business Week* Top 20 ranking
- The annual *Wall Street Journal* Top National Schools
- The annual *U.S. News & World Report* Top 20 ranking
- The biennial *Forbes* Top 60 Best Business Schools

A comparison of these rankings is shown in TABLE I (next page). A quick review shows striking differences in the rankings:

- Dartmouth is #1 in *The Wall Street Journal* and *Forbes* rankings, but was ranked only #10 by *Business Week* and #9 by *U.S. News.*
- Harvard and Stanford, two of the top business schools, are ranked in the Top 10 by *Business Week*, *U.S. News*, and *Forbes*, but only #14 and #15 by *The Wall Street Journal.*
- Iowa is ranked #12 by *Forbes* but doesn't appear in any of the other rankings.

There are many other dissimilarities across these rankings, but the point has been made: each publication has a different method and different criteria for ranking business schools.

Which ranking is best? To answer this question, we will examine how each publication calculates its business school ranking.

TABLE I: COMPARISON OF BUSINESS SCHOOL RANKINGS

Rank	BW 2004	WSJ 2005	US News 2006	Forbes 2005
1	Northwestern	Dartmouth	Harvard	Dartmouth
2	Chicago	Michigan	Stanford	Wharton
3	Wharton	Carnegie-Mellon	Wharton	Chicago
4	Stanford	Northwestern	MIT	Columbia
5	Harvard	Yale	Northwestern	Yale
6	Michigan	Wharton	Chicago	Stanford
7	Cornell	UC Berkeley	Columbia	Harvard
8	Columbia	Columbia	Berkeley	Virginia
9	MIT	North Carolina	Dartmouth	Cornell
10	Dartmouth	USC	UCLA	Northwestern
11	Duke	Virginia	Duke	Texas
12	Virginia	MIT	Michigan	Iowa
13	NYU	Chicago	NYU	NYU
14	UCLA	Harvard	Virginia	North Carolina
15	Carnegie-Mellon	Stanford	Yale	UC Berkeley
16	North Carolina	NYU	Carnegie-Mellon	Carnegie-Mellon
17	UC Berkeley	Duke	Cornell	Brigham Young
18	Indiana	Cornell	Emory	MIT
19	Texas	UCLA	Texas	UCLA
20	Emory		North Carolina	Duke
21			Purdue	Emory
22			Ohio State	Indiana
23			Indiana	Penn State
24			Michigan State	Texas A&M
25			Minnesota	Vanderbilt
26			Rochester	Michigan
27			Washington St. Louis	Washington St. Louis
28			Illinois	USC
29			USC	Maryland
30			U of Washington	Purdue
31			Texas A&M	SMU
32			Notre Dame	Michigan State
33			Wisconsin	Arizona
34			Arizona State	Ohio State
35			Brigham Young	Minnesota
36			Georgetown	Rochester
37			Georgia Tech	Georgetown
38			Penn State	UC Irvine
39			UC Irvine	William & Mary
40			Maryland	Wake Forest
41			Boston College	Rice
42			SMU	Wisconsin
43			Florida	Notre Dame
44			Boston University	Georgia
45			Rice	Georgia Tech
46			UC Davis	Boston U
47			Georgia	Rollins
48			Pittsburgh	SUNY Buffalo
49			Babson	South Carolina
50			Tulane	Florida
51			Vanderbilt	Tulane
52				Arizona State
53				Auburn
54				U of Washington
55				Oregon
56				Pepperdine
57				Boston College
58				UC Davis
59				Denver
60				Miami

The *Business Week* ranking

We begin with *Business Week*, the oldest and perhaps the most influential of the rankings. The *Business Week* ranking is based on a customer satisfaction survey with two main components:[49]

- An online survey of graduating MBA students. The students are asked to rate their school in 45 areas such as quality of teaching and effectiveness of the career services office on a 1 to 10 scale.
- An online survey of corporate recruiters who hire MBAs. The recruiters are requested to rank their top 20 schools in terms of student quality.

The *Business Week* survey has important limitations.

- Surveying students just before graduation is not the best time. Short-term irritations such as a low grade or difficulty finding the right job can cause a few students to give a school low marks, causing the student ratings of the school to plummet. This makes the student survey results very volatile from year to year. Asking the students their opinion about the quality of their education after they have been employed for a while would seem to have been a better choice.
- Because of the high volatility of responses from the student survey, the current data are smoothed by adding in data from earlier surveys. For example, the reported 2004 *Business Week* ranking contained 50% survey results from the Class of 2004 plus 25% from the Class of 2002 and 25% from the Class of 2000. Thus the

[49] For details, see "The Best Business Schools," *Business Week*, October 18, 2004.

reported student survey didn't necessarily reflect the state of the school in 2004.

- At many schools, graduating students are subjected to a certain amount of cheerleading by their dean before they respond to the *Business Week* survey. The dean reminds students that whatever they think of their experience in business school, their response will affect the ranking of the school and thus the perceived value of their degree in the marketplace.
- Only 223 companies that recruit MBAs responded to *Business Week's* recruiter survey in 2004. It is not clear how these companies were selected from the thousands of companies that hire MBAs. Are these few companies truly representative of the many industries and geographical locations where MBAs are hired?

Despite its limitations, the *Business Week* biennial ranking has been found to have a marked effect on how many students apply to a school. *Business Week* also maintains an excellent website that is chockfull of useful information for students shopping for a business school.

The *U.S. News & World Report* ranking

U.S. News & World Report takes a very different approach than *Business Week* to ranking business schools. Once a year, *U.S. News* publishes a special edition entitled "America's Best Graduate Schools."

The *U.S. News* rankings are produced by an entirely different methodology than the *Business Week* rankings. Instead of surveying just graduating students and corporate recruiters, the *U.S. News* rankings are compiled from a complex formula that includes surveys of business school deans, MBA program directors, and corporate recruiters; GMAT scores; starting salaries and signing bonuses; undergraduate grade point averages; and the percent of students employed at graduation and three months later. Various weightings are applied to these components to arrive at a total weighted score for each school, which then becomes the basis for the *U.S. News* ranking.[50]

Like the *Business Week* ranking, the *U.S. News* version also has limitations:

- How valid is the complex formula for picking programs that are most valuable to potential students? The calculation is a statistical stew ("add a little of this and a pinch of that"), but has it been shown to provide a useful measure of the value of each school?
- Are the schools always honest? When responding to *U.S. News*, do some schools leave out certain groups of students who might otherwise pull down the average GMAT scores and starting salaries they submit?
- Most deans and MBA program directors who are surveyed freely admit that of the more than 200 schools they are asked to rate, they are familiar with only a handful.
- As with the *Business Week* survey, how are the corporate recruiters selected? Are they representative of the many industries and geographic areas where MBAs are recruited?

---

[50] For more details, see *U.S. News and World Report*, America's Best Graduate Schools, 2007 edition, p. 21.

Despite these limitations, the *U.S. News* ranking has a wide following, and the articles that accompany the published rankings provide much useful information for prospective students.

The Wall Street Journal ranking

Every fall in late September, *The Wall Street Journal* publishes a business school ranking based entirely on ratings of the top schools by corporate recruiters.

The theory of *The Wall Street Journal* ranking is that recruiters who hire MBAs are the best judges of the quality of various programs.

This sounds plausible—until you look at the rankings and see some strange results. For example, Harvard and Stanford, arguably two of the best business schools, are ranked #14 and #15 (see TABLE I). *The Wall Street Journal* explains:

> "The most elite schools…suffer (in the ranking) from the fact that many recruiters come away empty-handed because the students are in such high demand."[51]

This statement suggests that what is good for recruiters is not always good for students, and vice versa. It calls into question the validity of *The Wall Street Journal* ranking as a guide for students seeking the best schools.

Another limitation of *The Wall Street Journal's* ranking is that it excludes small schools that might have programs of very high quality. Unless a school has at least 20 recruiters (and in practice, more like 50 or 60) who recruit there systematically, the school will not be eligible to be included. As a result, only 76 of the more

---

[51] Alsop, R., "Back on Top," *The Wall Street Journal*, September 21, 2005, p. R3.

than 400 business schools that are AACSB-accredited were included in the 2005 study.[52]

Given *The Wall Street Journal's* overall fine reputation as a publication, its ranking of business schools has influence. Although like other rankings, it has limitations, the information included in the articles that accompany the ranking can be very useful.

The *Forbes* ranking

In February 2000, *Forbes* introduced a new kind of business school ranking. Instead of relying on opinion surveys of graduates and recruiters, *Forbes* chose a more objective approach based on actual salary data.[53]

For the 2000 survey, *Forbes* sent questionnaires to more than 14,000 MBA graduates of the Class of 1994, inquiring about their salaries in the year before beginning business school, the first year out of school, and five years later.

Forbes then compared the total of five year's pay with an estimate of what the median student would have earned without the degree. After subtracting the investment cost (tuition and two years of foregone salary) and discounting the cash flows back to 1992, they derived the financial gain for an MBA for each of the schools.

This financial gain model was first developed in Yeaple, R.N., "The MBA Advantage," Adams Publishing, 1994 (see FIG. 2).

Forbes repeated the survey in 2001, 2003 and 2005. For the 2005 survey, *Forbes* expanded the survey to contacting 25,000

---

[52] Ibid. p. R5.

[53] "Measuring MBA Muscle," *Forbes*, February 7, 2000.

alumni from 111 MBA programs (see the *Forbes* methodology in Appendix A.)

The *Forbes* ranking has major advantages over other business school rankings:

- The primary advantage of the *Forbes* ranking is that it is based on what thousands of employers are willing to pay MBA graduates from the various schools, not only at the time of graduation but in the five years thereafter. Unlike the *Business Week*, *U.S. News*, and *Wall Street Journal* surveys, which are based on the subjective opinions of students and recruiters, the *Forbes* ranking is an objective measure based on actual salary data.

- The *Forbes* ranking does not discriminate against small schools, unlike the other surveys. Small schools with a high quality MBA program, for example, Rollins College, are included in the *Forbes* ranking.

- Beginning with the 2005 survey, *Forbes* ranks part-time as well as full-time programs. Since the majority of MBA students are part-timers, this is a useful feature found in no other business school rankings.

- The financial gain model methodology of the *Forbes* ranking is simple and straightforward. A potential student can estimate his or her personal financial gain from pursuing an MBA at various schools by entering a few numbers in an Excel spreadsheet (see Appendix B and C).

- As noted in an earlier chapter, the financial gains calculated by the *Forbes* ranking are consistent with other studies that estimate the lifetime value of an

MBA, such as that published by Davies and Cline.[54] Getting comparable answers using an entirely different methodology strongly suggests that the financial gains reported by *Forbes* are valid.

Like all rankings, the *Forbes* survey also has limitations:[55]

- The *Forbes* survey measures only one parameter of MBA education, financial gain. There are other reasons for pursuing an MBA, such as more career options, that are not covered in the *Forbes* ranking.
- Schools that place a high proportion of their students in high-paying first jobs, such as investment banking and top-level management consulting, tend to outperform other schools in the *Forbes* rankings.
- As with any survey, there is the possibility that those who respond may not be representative of the whole population of interest. For example, those MBA graduates who answer the *Forbes* survey may be more successful and have higher salaries than those who don't respond (market researchers call this non-response bias). Or they may submit numbers that are not truthful. But if such biases exist in the data—and there is no evidence that they do—they are likely to be consistent across all the schools. If so, they might change the magnitude of the financial gains reported but would not affect the ranking of schools.

---

[54] Davies, A. and Cline, T., "The ROI on the MBA," *BizEd*, January/February 2005, pp. 42-45.

[55] For a detailed statistical analysis of the advantages and limitations of the financial gain model that is the basis for the Forbes ranking, see Yeaple, R.N., "The MBA Advantage," Adams Publishing, 1994, pp. 264-287.

- The assumption in the *Forbes* version of the financial gain model about the alternative of not pursing an MBA—the line with the open dots in FIG. 2—is that the student's salary would grow at half the rate without an MBA as it would with an MBA. An alternative assumption is that the salary without an MBA would grow at a nominal rate of, say, 5% per year. As it turns out, the financial gain model is very robust with regard to this assumption. Although the magnitude of the financial gain changes across all the schools, the ranking of schools is largely insensitive to this assumption.[56]
- Finally, it must be emphasized that with all the rankings, the numbers that are reported are averages (or in some cases, medians). Those students who are talented and willing to work hard may do better than the reported averages. But those who do not put in the effort may not do as well.

The proliferation of business school rankings worries some business school faculty. Competition can be unsettling, particularly for those who have been sheltered in the ivory tower. They charge that the rankings are forcing schools to concentrate on trying to improve their standing in the rankings at the expense of investing in the long-run quality of their educational mission, particularly in the area of business research:

> "These rankings…sell magazines by promoting a public competition among business schools not unlike a horse race. Deans…face strong pressures to adopt 'quick fix, look good' curriculum revisions and other cosmetic changes that boost their schools' short-term ratings, but that

[56] Ibid., pp. 266-272.

> compromise their long-run mission to create and disseminate important new knowledge that benefits society."[57]

The value of business research is a complicated topic beyond the scope of this book. Historically, business research has contributed greatly to the quality of MBA education. At one time, giving students access to the latest research meant having them taught by those actually carrying out the research. It took years for new research findings to work their way through peer reviews, editing, and publication in the printed academic research journals.

But new technology such as the online Social Science Research Network has made the dissemination of research nearly instantaneous and costless. A faculty member does not have to do the research in order to present it in a timely manner to his or her students.

Moreover, if having students exposed for two years to cutting-edge research in the classroom is truly valuable, shouldn't this value show up as higher starting and early career salaries and bonuses for graduates of research-intensive schools? If so, these schools will have a decided advantage in rankings such as those conducted by *Forbes*.

Business school faculty are quick to point out that competition in the marketplace is good for consumers. Shouldn't this also apply to business schools? To the extent that at least some of the business school rankings—like the Powers rankings of new car quality—provide useful competitive information, they help promote such competition, and this is good for business schools and for prospective MBA students.

---

[57] DeAngelo, H., DeAngelo, L., and Zimmerman, J., "What's Really Wrong with U.S. Business Schools," 2005, available online as a preprint on the Social Science Research Network, www.ssrn.com.

Which survey is best? Each has its strengths and limitations. Prospective students would do well do review all of these surveys as well as the accompanying articles. Don't base your choice of school solely on the rankings. When you are ready to narrow your search, take the time to visit the campuses of your top two or three choices. Talk to current students and alumni. Sit in on a few classes. Call recruiters who hire graduates from these schools.

The bottom line is that the top schools are all excellent. Choosing among them is like choosing which model Lexus you would like to own. They may differ in style and features, but any of them would provide you with a superb education.

16

DARTMOUTH: A TOP-RANKED NATIONAL MBA PROGRAM

With more than 400 business schools accredited by the AACSB, prospective students have a wide choice.

Business schools can be divided into two broad groups: national schools that compete throughout the U.S and internationally for the best students, and regional schools that focus primarily on a more limited geographic area. Examples of two schools that provide exceptional five-year financial gains from teaching (Dartmouth and Rollins, see FIG. 5) are described in this section.

In 2005, the Tuck School of Business at Dartmouth College was ranked by both *Forbes* and *The Wall Street Journal* as the #1 business school in the U.S.[58] The Tuck School was also ranked #1 by *The Wall Street Journal* in 2001 and 2002.

As one of the leading business schools in the country, Tuck has developed a number of innovative strategies that contribute to its success:

- Collegiality and cooperation. Located along the Vermont border in Hanover, New Hampshire, hundreds of miles from the nearest large city, Tuck has turned its geographic remoteness into a virtue by emphasizing community, collegiality and cooperation among its students and faculty—characteristics that greatly impress corporate recruiters.[59]
- Outstanding teaching. Tuck takes teaching quality very seriously. As shown in FIG. 5, Dartmouth has been found by *Forbes* to offer the highest five-year financial gain of any U.S. business school, evidence of outstanding value-added by great teaching.
- Pioneering research. Although not a research powerhouse like the University of Chicago, in recent years Tuck has attracted world-class scholars such as Ken French, who is both a top researcher in finance and a first-rate teacher.
- Exclusively full-time MBA. Without the benefit of being located in a large metropolitan area, Tuck has no part-time MBA program, nor does it have an undergraduate business program. The School offers a number of executive

---

[58] Badenhausen, K. and Kump, L., "Best Business Schools," *Forbes*, September 5, 2005; "The Top Business Schools: Recruiters' Top Picks," *The Wall Street Journal*, September 21, 2005.

[59] "The Top Business Schools: Recruiters' Top Picks," *The Wall Street Journal*, September 21, 2005.

education short courses but does not have a degree-granting Executive MBA program. Unlike almost all other top business schools, Tuck does not have a Ph.D. program. All of its resources are directed into refining and improving its full-time MBA program.

- Cultivation of the alumni. Founded in 1900, Tuck was the first graduate school of business in the country. The School stays in close contact with its graduates and takes pride in its alumni giving rate of 64%, the highest of any business school.
- Virtuous cycle. As explained by Senior Associate Dean Robert Hansen, Tuck has established a "virtuous cycle" of alumni hiring graduates into high paying jobs. Most jobs are not the result of on-campus interviewing, but rather through networking with alumni, particularly in the fields of investment banking and management consulting.
- Small school. Finally, Tuck is one of the smallest of the national business schools, which contributes to its culture of collegiality and collaboration.

17

ROLLINS: A HIGHLY-RANKED INNOVATIVE REGIONAL MBA PROGRAM

Everyone understands that an MBA from Dartmouth or Harvard is a good investment. But what about an MBA from a high-quality regional school?

The Roy E. Crummer Graduate School of Business is part of Rollins College, a small high-quality liberal arts college in Winter Park, Florida that was recently ranked by *U.S. News and World Report* as the #1 regional university in the South.[60]

Although smaller than most leading business schools, the Crummer School provides financial gains comparable to many larger and better known business schools. Note, for example, that

[60] "America's Best Colleges 2006," *U.S. News & World Report*, August 22, 2005.

in FIG. 7 Rollins is located just below the midpoint in the listing of a selection of leading business schools.

In the 2005 *Forbes* survey based on the value of the MBA degree, the full-time Rollins MBA was ranked #1 in Florida and #47 nationally, which places it in the top 12% of AACSB-accredited U.S. business schools. The part-time program was ranked #14 nationally.

Under the leadership of Dean Craig McAllaster, the Crummer School has developed several innovative strategies to provide exceptional value for its students:

- Emphasis on great teaching. Unlike most leading business schools, Crummer hires only experienced faculty who have developed their teaching skills somewhere else, and have a track record of exceptional teaching. There are no assistant professors or graduate teaching assistants on the Rollins MBA faculty, only associate and full professors. Furthermore, unlike other business schools, all of these experienced teachers are hired without tenure, which is granted only after several years when they have proved they are able to meet the School's high standards for teaching.

  In addition to strong academic credentials—all of the regular faculty have doctorates—most have extensive industry and consulting experience, which insures that classroom discussions address real business problems.

  Evidence for the effectiveness of Crummer's superior teaching is provided in FIGS. 5 and 6, where Rollins is positioned well "above the line."

- Smaller classes. The class size in the core courses at most leading business schools is about 75 students. At Rollins, the maximum class size in the core courses is 40 students, providing a closer, more intimate learning environment. Students get to really know their professors and their classmates, and everyone has plenty of opportunities to contribute to class discussions.

- Textbooks, not academic journals. Again, unlike most leading business schools, the Rollins MBA faculty are not pressured to publish in refereed academic journals. Rather, the faculty publish mainly textbooks—a measure of their ability to transform abstract research findings into practical material that is useful in the classroom—again, a dimension of their commitment to teaching.

- Exclusively MBA. The Crummer School is one of only a few leading business schools that focus exclusively on graduate business education. Many business schools have huge undergraduate programs that often dwarf their MBA programs, which can be a distraction for faculty that are required to teach in both programs.

- Younger full-time students. Unlike most leading business schools, Crummer has pioneered in accepting bright students who have little or no pre-MBA work experience. As a result, while its average pre-MBA salaries are lower because its students are younger, its average five-year financial gain—a measure of value-added by the program—is comparable to that of other high quality MBA programs, as evidenced by its standing in the 2005 *Forbes* ranking.

- A full range of programs for part-time students. With an unemployment rate of only 2.8%, the Greater Orlando area is growing and thriving.[61] This provides the opportunity

[61] "In the 49 metropolitan areas with a Census 2000 population of 1 million or more, the lowest December jobless rates (was) reported in Orlando, Fla., 2.8

for the Crummer School to offer a full range of MBA programs for part-timers:

- A traditional two-year evening program that meets twice a week and can be completed in 32 months. The average age of students is 29.
- A recently introduced all-day Saturday program that can be completed in only 22 months. These students average 34 years of age.
- An executive MBA program for senior managers, average age 38, that also can be completed in 22 months.

All of these part-time courses are taught by the same faculty that has brought distinction to the School's full-time MBA program.

The success of the Rollins MBA provides evidence that a high-quality regional business school with an innovative strategy can offer five-year financial gains comparable to those of well-known national schools.

When considering a regional school, look for AACSB accreditation, small class sizes, and an experienced senior faculty that places teaching quality first.

---

percent," *Metropolitan Area Employment and Unemployment Summary*, Bureau of Labor Statistics, February 1, 2006.

18

SOME CLOSING THOUGHTS ON WHETHER IT PAYS TO GET AN MBA

As we saw in the graph in FIG. 1 at the beginning of this book, the MBA degree has been a major success story for higher education because graduates have found that it is worth the investment in time and money. Some final thoughts about the value of the degree…

- There are many reasons to pursue an MBA degree—financial gain is just one.
- It pays to choose a high-quality school, one accredited by the AACSB.
- The *Forbes* 2005 survey data shows that students can earn substantial financial rewards by earning an MBA at these leading schools.
- A part-time degree can be just as valuable as a full-time degree.
- Keep in mind that the financial gain numbers shown are averages, and not every student will be this successful. Some, of course, will do better.

- Finally, recognize that to maximize your personal gain from getting an MBA, you will have to work hard, not only on the coursework but also on getting the best possible job when you graduate. The value of *your* MBA will depend on how much effort you are willing to put into it.

Business has become too complex and too competitive to wing it. If you are serious about a career in management, the education and the credentials of the MBA are invaluable.

The world of business is changing rapidly. It's fashionable these days to talk about "the learning organization." But organizations don't learn; people do. And lifelong learning will be greatly enhanced by a thorough grounding in the fundamentals, which is best acquired through the formal process of education. To paraphrase Louis Pasteur:

"Change favors the prepared mind."

In closing, I wish you the very best of luck in your career!

APPENDICES

APPENDIX A: METHODOLOGY OF THE *FORBES* 2005 BUSINESS SCHOOL SURVEY

Forbes

Best Business Schools

Methodology

08.18.05, 6:00 PM ET

Our rankings of business schools are based on the return on investment that graduates of the Class of 2000 received.

We sent surveys to 25,000 alumni of 111 M.B.A. programs around the world and heard back from 24% of them.

We asked for their pre-M.B.A. salaries as well as compensation figures for three of the first five years after getting their degrees. We compared their post-M.B.A. compensation with their opportunity cost (tuition and forgone salary while in school) and what they would have made had they stayed in their old jobs.

We adjusted salary figures to account for cost-of-living expenses and discounted the earnings gains, using a rate tied to money market yields.[62]

---

[62] Badenhausen, K. and Kump, L., "Best Business Schools," *Forbes*, September 5, 2005, p. 152.

APPENDIX B: SPREADSHEET FOR ESTIMATING THE VALUE OF A FULL-TIME MBA

	Assumptions
Pre-MBA pay	35,000
Growth rate without MBA	5%
Tuition per year (less scholarships, etc.)	20,000
Post-MBA starting salary	60,000
Signing bonus (at graduation)	10,000
Post-MBA growth rate	15%
Discount rate (money market rate)	4%

Year	Pay without MBA	Salary with MBA	Bonuses	Total Pay with MBA	Difference	Cum Difference	Discounted Gain
0	35,000	35,000		35,000	0	0	0
1	36,750	-20,000		-20,000	-56,750	-56,750	-54,567
2	38,588	-20,000		-20,000	-58,588	-115,338	-54,167
3	40,517	60,000	10,000	70,000	29,483	-85,854	26,210
4	42,543	69,000		69,000	26,457	-59,397	22,616
5	44,670	79,350		79,350	34,680	-24,717	28,505
6	46,903	91,253		91,253	44,349	19,632	35,050
7	49,249	104,940		104,940	55,692	75,324	42,321
					Five-year Gain =	**75,324**	**45,967**

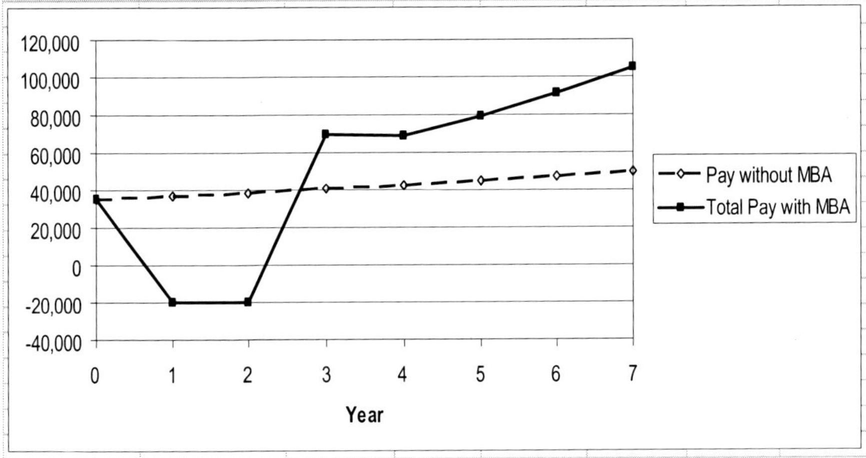

NOTES FOR THE **FULL-TIME** SPREADSHEET

1. This Excel spreadsheet shows the discounted five-year financial gain = $57,240 for the example using the values listed in the Assumptions section at the top of the spreadsheet.

2. You can develop your own personal version of this Five-Year Financial Gain Model for a full-time MBA by using the formulas shown on the next page. Then insert your own values for Pre-MBA Pay, etc. in the Assumptions section of the spreadsheet.

3. If you expect bonuses every year, enter these values directly into the spreadsheet.

4. If you plan to work part-time while in school, reduce the Tuition by your part-time pay.

5. By changing the values in the Assumptions section, you can show how sensitive the five-year financial gain value is to various assumptions.

FORMULAS FOR THE FULL-TIME MBA SPREADSHEET

	A	B	C	D	E	F	G	H
1			**Assumptions**					
2	Pre-MBA pay		35000					
3	Growth rate without MBA		0.05					
4	Tuition per year (less scholarships, etc.)		20000					
5	Post-MBA starting salary		60000					
6	Signing bonus (at graduation)		10000					
7	Post-MBA growth rate		0.15					
8	Discount rate (money market rate)		0.04					
9								
10								
11								
12	**Year**	**Pay without MBA**	**Salary with MBA**	**Bonuses**	**Total Pay with MBA**	**Difference**	**Cum Difference**	**Discounted Gain**
13	0	=C2	=C2		=C13+D13	=E13-B13	=F13	=F13/((1+C8)^A13)
14	1	=B13*(1+C3)	=-1*C4		=C14+D14	=E14-B14	=G13+F14	=F14/((1+C8)^A14)
15	2	=B14*(1+C3)	=-1*C4		=C15+D15	=E15-B15	=G14+F15	=F15/((1+C8)^A15)
16	3	=B15*(1+C3)	=C5	=C6	=C16+D16	=E16-B16	=G15+F16	=F16/((1+C8)^A16)
17	4	=B16*(1+C3)	=C16*(1+C7)		=C17+D17	=E17-B17	=G16+F17	=F17/((1+C8)^A17)
18	5	=B17*(1+C3)	=C17*(1+C7)		=C18+D18	=E18-B18	=G17+F18	=F18/((1+C8)^A18)
19	6	=B18*(1+C3)	=C18*(1+C7)		=C19+D19	=E19-B19	=G18+F19	=F19/((1+C8)^A19)
20	7	=B19*(1+C3)	=C19*(1+C7)		=C20+D20	=E20-B20	=G19+F20	=F20/((1+C8)^A20)
21								
22						**Five-year Gain =**	**=G20**	**=SUM(H13:H21)**
23								
24								

25 26 27 28 29 30 31 32 33 34 35 36 37 38 39 40 41 42

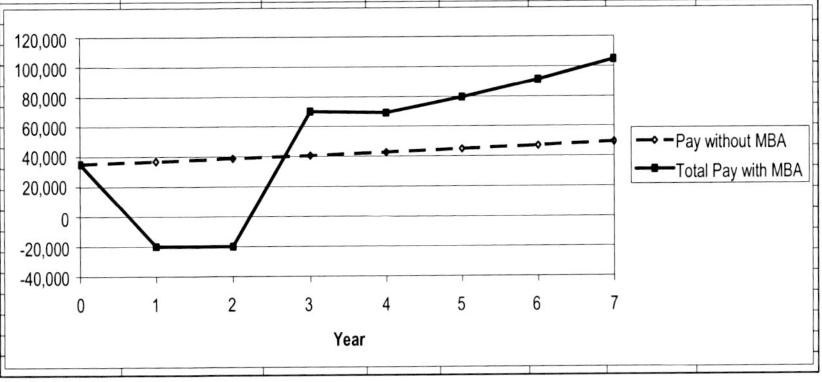

APPENDIX C: SPREADSHEET FOR ESTIMATING THE VALUE OF A PART-TIME MBA

	Assumptions
Pre-MBA pay	35,000
Growth rate without MBA	5%
Tuition per year (less scholarships, etc.)	20,000
Post-MBA starting salary	60,000
Signing bonus (at graduation)	0
Post-MBA growth rate	15%
Discount rate (money market rate)	4%

Year	Pay without MBA	Salary with MBA	Bonuses	Total Pay with MBA	Difference	Cum Difference	Discounted Gain
0	35,000	35,000		35,000	0	0	0
1	36,750	16,750		16,750	-20,000	-20,000	-19,231
2	38,588	18,588		18,588	-20,000	-40,000	-18,491
3	40,517	60,000	0	60,000	19,483	-20,517	17,320
4	42,543	69,000		69,000	26,457	5,940	22,616
5	44,670	79,350		79,350	34,680	40,621	28,505
6	46,903	91,253		91,253	44,349	84,970	35,050
7	49,249	104,940		104,940	55,692	140,662	42,321
					Five-year Gain =	**140,662**	**108,090**

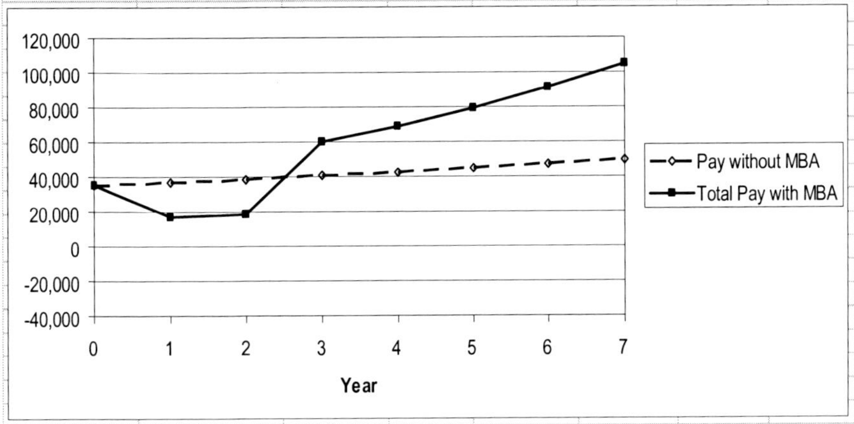

NOTES FOR THE **PART-TIME** SPREADSHEET

1. In this spreadsheet, "Pay without the MBA" continues during the two years in school.
2. Many part-time and executive MBA programs can be completed in 2 years. If a part-time program will continue for 3 years or more, the formulas (next page) can be modified.
3. No signing bonus is included in the part-time spreadsheet because it is assumed that part-time students will continue to work for their current employer after graduation.
4. If an employer pays part or all of the tuition, only the part paid by the student should be entered in the Assumptions.
5. With the exception of the signing bonus, the assumptions in this part-time spreadsheet are the same as those in the full-time spreadsheet, but the financial gain is higher because there is no opportunity cost of foregone salary.

FORMULAS FOR THE PART-TIME MBA SPREADSHEET

	A	B	C	D	E	F	G	H
1			**Assumptions**					
2	Pre-MBA pay		35000					
3	Growth rate without MBA		0.05					
4	Tuition per year (less scholarships, etc.)		20000					
5	Post-MBA starting salary		60000					
6	Signing bonus (at graduation)		0					
7	Post-MBA growth rate		0.15					
8	Discount rate (money market rate)		0.04					
9								
10								
11								
12	**Year**	**Pay without MBA**	**Salary with MBA**	**Bonuses**	**Total Pay with MBA**	**Difference**	**Cum Difference**	**Discounted Gain**
13	0	=C2	=C2		=C13+D13	=E13-B13	=F13	=F13/((1+C8)^A13)
14	1	=B13*(1+C3)	=B14-1*C4		=C14+D14	=E14-B14	=G13+F14	=F14/((1+C8)^A14)
15	2	=B14*(1+C3)	=B15-1*C4		=C15+D15	=E15-B15	=G14+F15	=F15/((1+C8)^A15)
16	3	=B15*(1+C3)	=C5	=C6	=C16+D16	=E16-B16	=G15+F16	=F16/((1+C8)^A16)
17	4	=B16*(1+C3)	=C16*(1+C7)		=C17+D17	=E17-B17	=G16+F17	=F17/((1+C8)^A17)
18	5	=B17*(1+C3)	=C17*(1+C7)		=C18+D18	=E18-B18	=G17+F18	=F18/((1+C8)^A18)
19	6	=B18*(1+C3)	=C18*(1+C7)		=C19+D19	=E19-B19	=G18+F19	=F19/((1+C8)^A19)
20	7	=B19*(1+C3)	=C19*(1+C7)		=C20+D20	=E20-B20	=G19+F20	=F20/((1+C8)^A20)
21								
22						**Five-year Gain =**	**=G20**	**=SUM(H13:H21)**
23								
24								

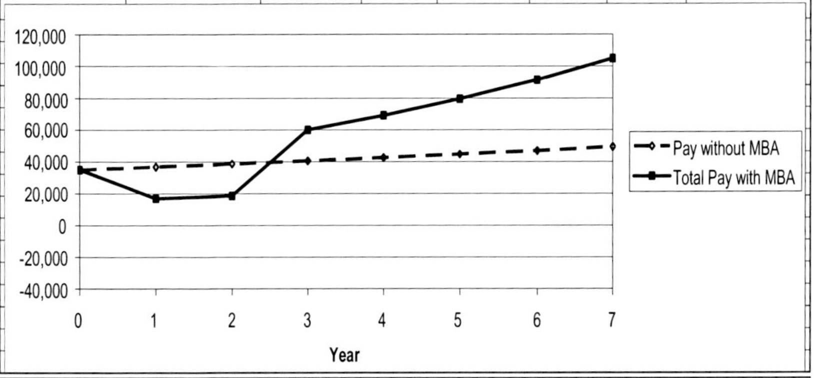

INDEX

NOTES